Can You Find It?

Spooky Sights

A Can-You-Find-It Book

by Sarah L. Schuette

T0021105

PEBBLE
a capstone imprint

Eye See You!

Can you find these things?

candy

fish bones

red pepper

star

wand   pig   dragonfly   tongs   pineapple   cupcake

Full Moon

Can you find these things?

witch hat

tire

horseshoe

sword

 watermelon

 oar

 airplane

 dragon

 alligator

 grill

Zombie Lunch

Can you find these things?

book

flamingo

eggplant

butterfly

 snake

 toaster

 blender

 light bulb

 rainbow

 pickle

Boo!

Can you find
these things?

hand

corn
cob

wizard
hat

grapes

mushroom

palm tree

race car

snowflake

tractor

cactus

Haunted House

Can you find
these things?

 balloon

 pencil

 chicken

 snowman

penguin

trophy

comb

hair
dryer

bone

arrow

Skeleton Dance

Can you find these things?

umbrella   strawberry   hanger   cow

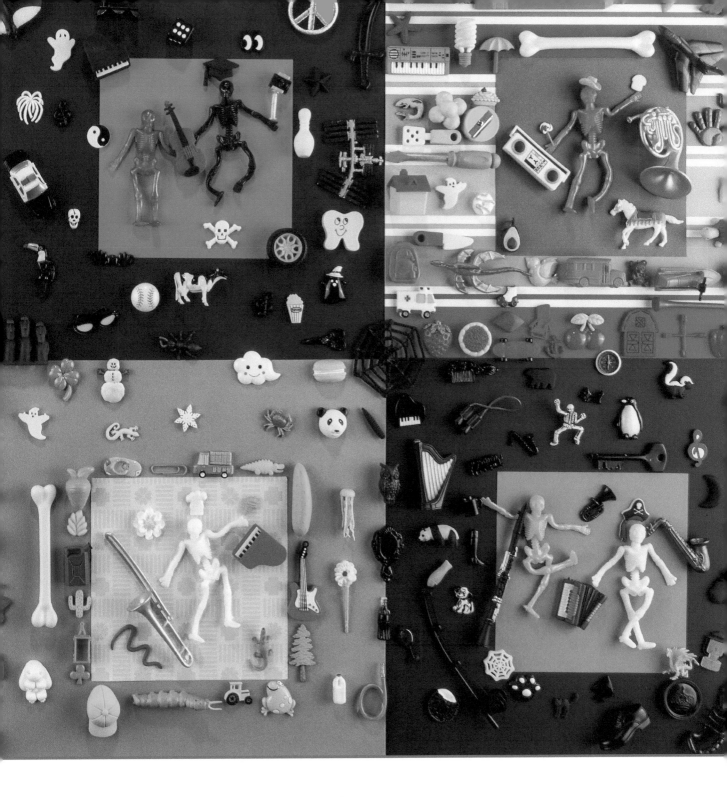

 skunk

 hot dog

 sunglasses

 basketball

 snake

seahorse

Monster Mouths

Can you find these things?

drill

koala

stapler

globe

 paintbrush

 shell

 rabbit

 knife

 mitten

 scooter

Mummy Madness

Can you find these things?

 lion

 swan

 football

 donut

 ladder

 chef's hat

 french fries

 rooster

 clothespin

dog

Jack-o-Lanterns

Can you find these things?

teddy bear

starfish

bananas

gnome

taco

candy
corn

rubber
duck

soda

ninja

tiger

Spells and Potions

Can you find these things?

pretzel

turtle

bat

taxi

 bowling pin

 bobber

 bucket

 calculator

 peanut

 skull

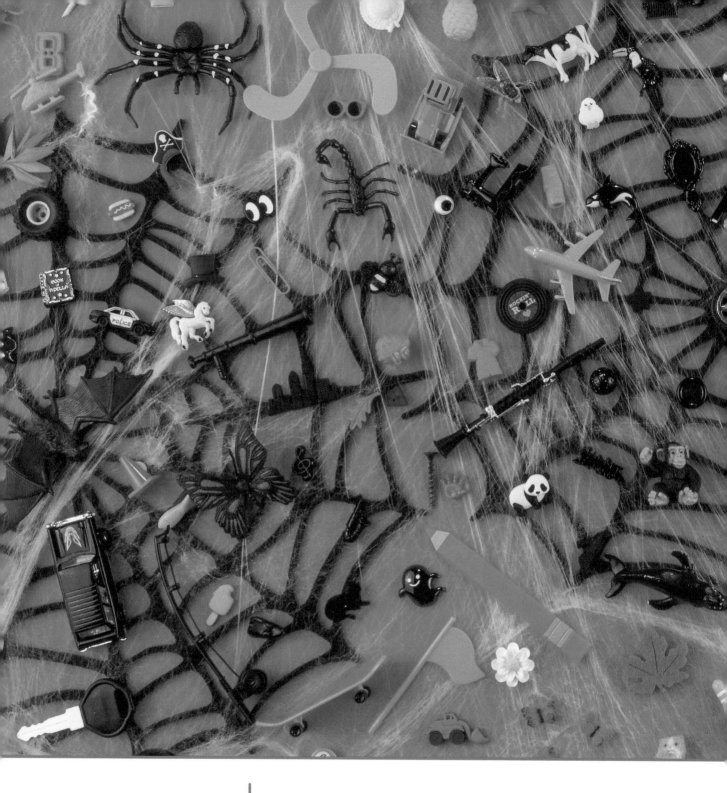

Webs

Can you find
these things?

octopus

pizza

fly

ice pop

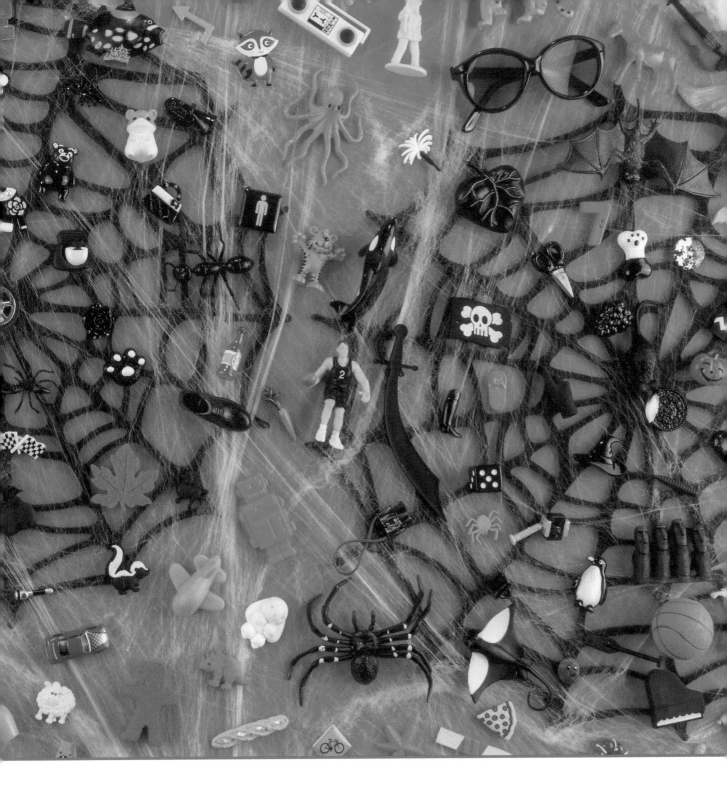

 helicopter

 shirt

 scissors

 panda

 traffic cone

carrot

Wolves in the Woods

Can you find
these things?

hamburger

ax

spoon

shark

camel

pants

rolling
pin

wrench

zipper

tent

Wicked Witch

Can you find
these things?

 ant

 clarinet

 compass

 harp

 gorilla

 lobster

 mouse

 crown

 robot

 trash can

Challenge Puzzle

Infested!

Can you find
these things?

key

donkey

leaf

moon

PETTING ZOO

Turn the page for the answer key!

pumpkin

baseball bat

shoe

cat

crutch

snail

Psst! Did you know that Pebs the Pebble was hiding
in EVERY PUZZLE in this book?

It's true! Go back and look! Hi.

Look for other books in this series:

The author dedicates this book to the Harper Family.

Pebble Sprout is published by Pebble, an imprint of Capstone.
1710 Roe Crest Drive, North Mankato, Minnesota 56003
www.capstonepub.com

Copyright © 2021 by Capstone. All rights reserved. No part of this publication may be reproduced in whole or in part, or stored in a retrieval system, or transmitted in any form or by any means, electronic, mechanical, photocopying, recording, or otherwise, without written permission of the publisher.

Library of Congress Cataloging-in-Publication Data is available on the Library of Congress website.
ISBN 978-1-9771-2256-8 (library binding)
ISBN 978-1-9771-2622-1 (paperback)
ISBN 978-1-9771-2308-4 (eBook PDF)

Summary: Lead kids on a tour of spooky sights! Zombies, witches, monsters, and other spine-chilling creatures make finding the hidden objects in the full-color photo puzzles a BOO-tastic challenge. Pictographs and word labels are included in each to-find list.

Image Credits
All photos by Capstone Studio: Karon Dubke

Editorial Credits
Shelly Lyons, editor; Heidi Thompson, designer; Marcy Morin, set stylist; Morgan Walters, media researcher; Kathy McColley, production specialist